JEWELS
AND RULES

(42 act of chivalry)

KAREEM GALATHE

Dedicated to

My three daughters (queens),

Empress Menen, Malaya Symone, and Ja'Sira Vi.

Their future is my present. To be blessed with daughters is by far the greatest experience I've ever known.

Remember The 3 A's In A Relationship. 1. Attention 2. Appreciation. 3. Affection

The successful running of a relationship is often a combination of crucial factors. None can operate without the other! A man needs to show his woman attention the same way he needs to appreciate her being as well as shower affection on her. In the same vein, a woman also needs to reciprocate attention, appreciation, and affection with her man. When both relationship partners are committed to exuding these three virtues towards one another, there's no stopping them in the heights of love they would attain.

Most Men Aren't Smart Enough To Realize That The Higher You Elevate Your Woman, The Less Valuable She Is To Other Men. When You Break Her Down, You Make Her Accessible To Anyone She Thinks Will Treat Her Better.

Being in a relationship comes with several premonitions. One of such strong ones is the thought that you are better off with someone else. Such thought visits even those in the most romantic of relationships at times, so you'll understand that what keeps you in a relationship above all else is trust. Trust your woman and keep her feeling like the only woman on earth, then see if other men will give her serenades to get her heart. It would be too apparent to them that she is so into you. But when you begin to make her feel like she is a piece of trash by having no regard for her in a relationship, it opens room for men who can treat her like a queen to steal her heart away.

She Loves Her Independence, And Yet Sometimes And Likes To Be Told What To Do. That's Part Of Her Contradiction And Part Of Her Magic, And Part Of Your Magic Will Be When You Understand.

In a relationship, a man has got to understand the place of independence in the woman's life. One should not act all bossy in the relationship and take her power of decision-making in the process. Preferably, a man has to make sure he allows her to be what she wants to be and that the relationship is not a stumbling block to her ambitions. On the other hand, a man should learn to be a guide to his woman in the chosen direction of her interest. He should not act domineeringly to make her do things she does not want to do. Instead, he should let her make mistakes at times and learn from them, while he guides her and is there for her through her dream walk.

The Way You Treat Her At The Very Beginning When You Were Trying To Get Her Should Be The Way You Always Treat Her, Don't Change

After getting a woman, most men start to slip away gradually from their commitment towards her. They do not express the same romantic nature they had before the chase. It is a common experience women relate to, especially in marriage. Most women admit that the courtship phase is the most romantic part of their life. Be the man who remains committed to making his woman happy by loving her even much more during marriage than engagement. As a single man, also learn to show love equally as you had shown when you were not in a relationship with her yet.

When You Date A Real Man, You'll Get The "Don't Worry Baby I Got It," "Let's Go...Let's Do It...I Planned This For Us" Instead Of Dealing With "Sorry, I Forgot, I Can't Make It, Not Today" "You Didm't Text Me First." "I Was Busy," "Sorry For Not Texting You All Day' Kind Of Man.

Experiences in relationship depend on the kind of man you are dating, as a female. It is the very reason you have to be careful when dating a man. A man who values his woman would see a possibility in any idea she brings up to him. He would be up to it; directing her on the best way to manage her idea for optimum productivity. That's a real man. A man who does not take delight in the progress of his woman does not show that he loves her and deserves her love in return.

Connection Doesn't Care About The Laws Of Your Land. Your Soul Would Be Pulled To The Places It Belongs

Often, the most romantic of relationships occur between individuals of different cultural heritages, religion, races, and other defining elements. And that's because true love requires two people committed to giving happiness a chance in their relations with each other. Love is worth fighting for, irrespective of sentimental barriers of individual differences and heritages. Once you see the one for whom your heart beats for, you'll be drawn from the depth of your souls into such person and be uneasy until you blurt out your feelings for him or her and get it reciprocated.

What Attracts A Man's Attention Does Not Always Attract His Respect.

It is a common knowledge that men are moved by sight; hence, they are easily attracted by beautiful faces, curves, and other alluring properties of women. Despite this, men do not always go for people whom they have features about that they admire. Instead, they'll die to be with a lady who makes them feel like the man they are. It is this internal principle in men that makes them different from animals who are moved by the whims of their emotions to chase every oppositely-sexed one they find in their way. Not everything that gets a man's attention gets his respect!

Something I Heard While Growing Up: Girls, Boys Mature More Slowly That You. Make Allowance For Them. Something I Never Heard: Boys, Girls Mature More Rapidly Than You. Look To Them As Examples Of Intelligence And Leadership

More often than not, the understanding of female and male development is lacking in relationships. Nearly all relationship problems are misunderstandings of the concept that men and women operate on. If all men understood that their women are faster developers and can modestly seek to understand their perspective, it would go a long way in aiding their relationship. On the converse, a woman who understands the place of slower development for her man should be tolerant of allowing him to grow to understand her, or slow enough to explain whatever he finds difficult to understand. That is what relationships are all about – mutual understanding.

Money Does Not Make A Man. Muscles Does Not Make A Man. Tattoos Do Not Make A Man. Character Is What Makes A Man. Let A Man's Character Be His Currency That Will Tell You What He Is Worth.

The earmarks of a man are not his physique, fleets of cars or houses, possessions and all. In this contemporary age, there are equally as many women who possess these material things as well. However, what makes a man respected by a woman in the most profound sense is his strength of character. Every woman wants a man that she can vouch for; someone she can cross her heart that he would always be there when she needs him. Having cars or houses and other earthly items of ostentation does not cover for the character. Therefore, as a man, endeavor to build a name in the heart of your woman through the building blocks of ethical conduct.

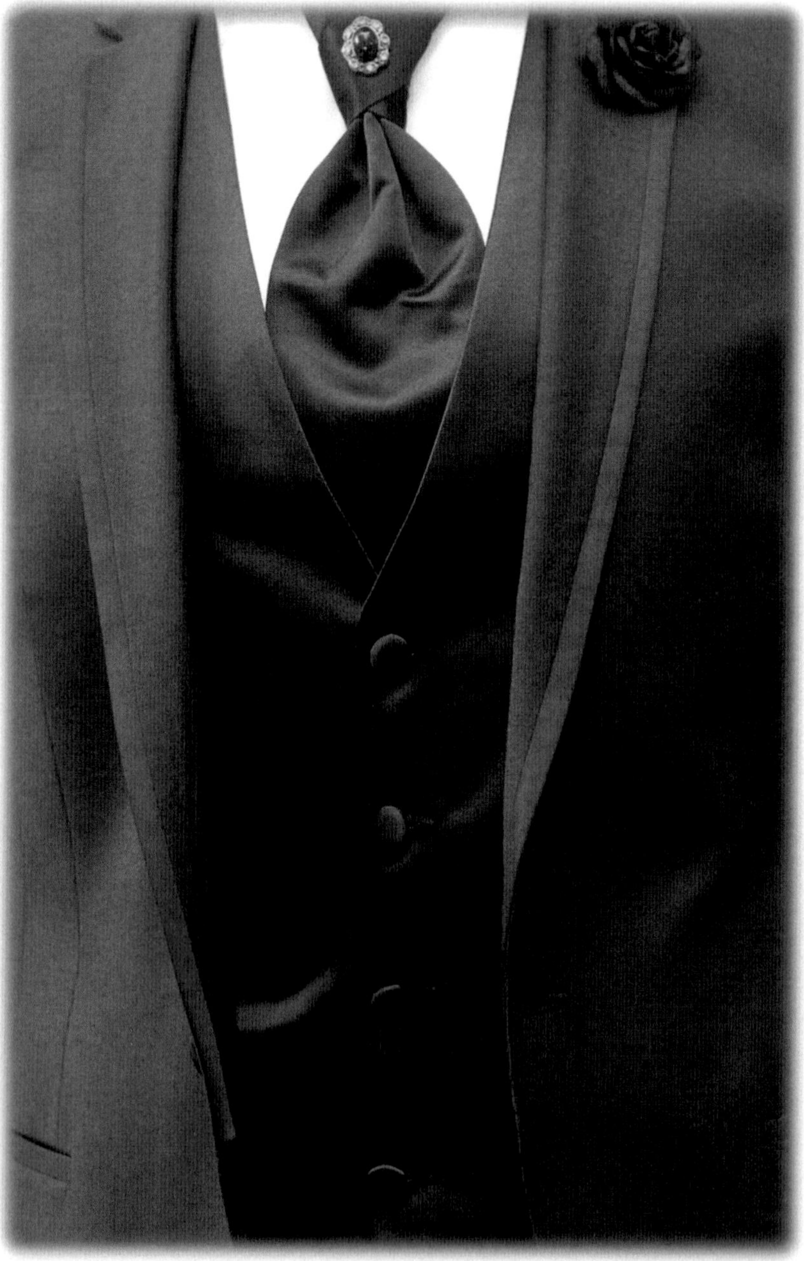

A Gentleman Will Open Doors, Pull Out Chairs, Carry Things. Not Because She Is Helpless Or Unable, But Because He Wants To Show Her That She Is Valuable And Worthy Of Respect

To open doors, pull out chairs, and and other chivalric things are a signs of kindness. Sadly, many today see it as a sign of slavery on the part of the man. Some women even do not consent to such courteous behavior because they think they are perceived as weak when such gestures are shown. Acts of chivalry as there is not a sign of weakness or slavery. Instead, it is a sign of honor for the one a man claims to love. Such seed planted in the heart of a woman will never be forgotten as she will treat you as her god in every way.

Its Very Rare To Find Someone That Genuinely Cares About You, That Wants To See You Achieve All Your Goals, That Wants To Help You Grow As A Person And Be By Your Side At Every Step Of The Way. If You Have That Kind Of Person Don't Let Them Go. It Is Rare To Find.

The ancient maxim has it that a bird at hand is worth many in the bush. So many people let go of real love with the idea that another person would show them the same love. It occurs mostly when the person meets love at a time that he or she is not ready financially or otherwise to accommodate the love entreaty. However, most great marriages today started from youthful days of not having it all. Hence one should also learn to grow in love while waiting for the desired change to come. Letting go of love as a result of lack is never the best option. True love is hard to find!

Kiss Her Randomly, When She Least Expects It

Getting into your woman is the best thing any man can do. The benefits that come with it are numerous. Foreplay actions like kisses go a long way to making her feel loved. As her man, make sure to kiss your woman anywhere and everywhere. Kiss her on her face, hands and anywhere imaginable. When a woman sees a passionate kiss, she recognizes love and reciprocates it to the man. A kiss does not always have to lead to sex. Make kissing your language of love that translates to "I love you."

Sometimes You Meet Someone Who Can Change Everything

In the journey of love, you will meet people who do not mean well for you as well as those who mean well for you. You will encounter snakes as well as doves. A few may be lucky never to have love ordeals, but many can relate to having one bad experience or the other. When you come out of a bad relationship, you should learn to separate your ex from your definition of love. There is always a silver lining in the sky. That means you can experience good, even after a bad relationship. Hence always believe that true love exists and be ready to wait for it till it comes. Avoid rushing into a relationship under pressure or forming negative schemas about love after romantic setbacks and your dream woman or man will come your way.

Love Is A Verb: Make Sure Your Actions Speak Louder Than Your Words

One of the most said clause of all time is "I love you." Many times, it is not meant the way it is reported. Love is a verb that means that it involves you doing things to show it. It is not about saying you love a person; your actions to the person will let the person know of a truth that you love him or her. In the same vein, acts of love like calling her often, enjoying to be by her, caring for her needs and other expressions of love are enough to make a woman feel loved far much effectively than telling her you to love her.

Yes, They Come Back Because Your Energy Is Amazing. They Also Come Back Because They Want More Free Access To It.

Why would a woman might want to come back to a man despite leaving him. It is common these days to find exes come back to their lovers despite even being in new relationships. The reason is they enjoy the energy they got from you. Hence you must be willing to define your relationships with people and stop giving energy to exes who do not regard you as a lover anymore. That way, you will be able to avoid complicated relationships and be true to your feelings, then recognizing true love any time it comes.

When Her Mind Is Stroked, Her Body Talks Differently.

Pleasuring a woman is something that many men take to mean making physical touches and attempts to caress her. While this is partly true, it also follows that a man that has not gotten a woman's heart cannot get the right response from her body. Even when he wants to have sexual relations with her, she could feel violated, and that is because she does not feel a soul connection. Therefore men should understand the rule of thumb for pleasuring a woman and getting her cooperation in everything – satisfy her mind and her body will be yours.

Females That Look Mean Have The Best Personalities. You Just Have To Know How To Break The Ice.

Many times, men tend to avoid women who have mean looking countenances when looking around to make love overtures to a lady. They get scared of what they think would be her reaction if they said hello to her. Whereas the converse is the reality most of the time – women with a dour expression on their faces tend to be people with some of the best personalities you can ever imagine. Most times, insecurities may make a woman assume a closed body language or some mind issues bothering her at the time. When she is in that mood, you need to be in a sanguine mood to get to her and bring her mood up. As a man, you need to have the perfect ice breaker to get into her, and you'd be amazed how addicted she would get to you in a short while.

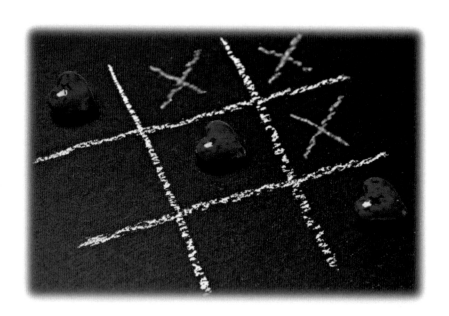

A King Does Not Choose A Lazy Queen. A Girl Without Goals Of Her Own Is A Liability. A Woman That Keeps You Focused Along With Her Own Is An Asset

As a man, you need a woman who keeps you on course with your life ambition since she chases hers. Don't be the kind of woman who is just about what she can get from a relationship. Rather be a contributor to the relationship – it increases your value in the eyes of your man. Every man wants an asset and not a liability. Be that woman with a high sense of industry, and your man will forever appreciate your essence in his life.

Cuddle Often. Kiss A Lot. Be Naughty. Have A Lot Of Dirty Sex. Love Deeply. Be Happy.

The feelings of love initially experienced at the beginning of a relationship sometimes wane at different points in a relationship. However, the fire of intimacy is what sustains a relationship through the different phases. Romance is not overrated. Kissing, cuddling, and dirty sex is what helps to build two lovers into themselves. That is what makes lovers intricately intertwined into themselves. When you do not access the intimate space of your woman, you give room for love to be lost in your relationship.

Soulmate: A Person With Whom You Have An Immediate Connection With The Moment You Meet – A Connection So Strong That You Are Drawn To Them In A Way You Have Never Experienced Before. As This Connection Develops Over Time, You Experience Love So Deep, Strong And Complex, That You Begin To Doubt That You Have Ever Truly Loved Anyone Prior. Your Soulmate Understands And Connects With You On Every Way And On Every Level, Which Brings A Sense Of Peace, Calmness, And Happiness When You Are Around Them.

Many things the idea of a soulmate is a fictional character in fairy tales –one who never exists in reality. However, that is not true. Although there is not one person who passes for a soulmate, he or she is someone who understands one's physical, emotional, and spiritual nature and has chemistry with them. A soulmate does not necessarily have to come in the picture of your dream lover exactly. However, he or she is someone you find easily connecting with at all times, which is not ready to take you for granted. He or she outclasses all romantic experiences you have had before. Such a person is none other but your soulmate!

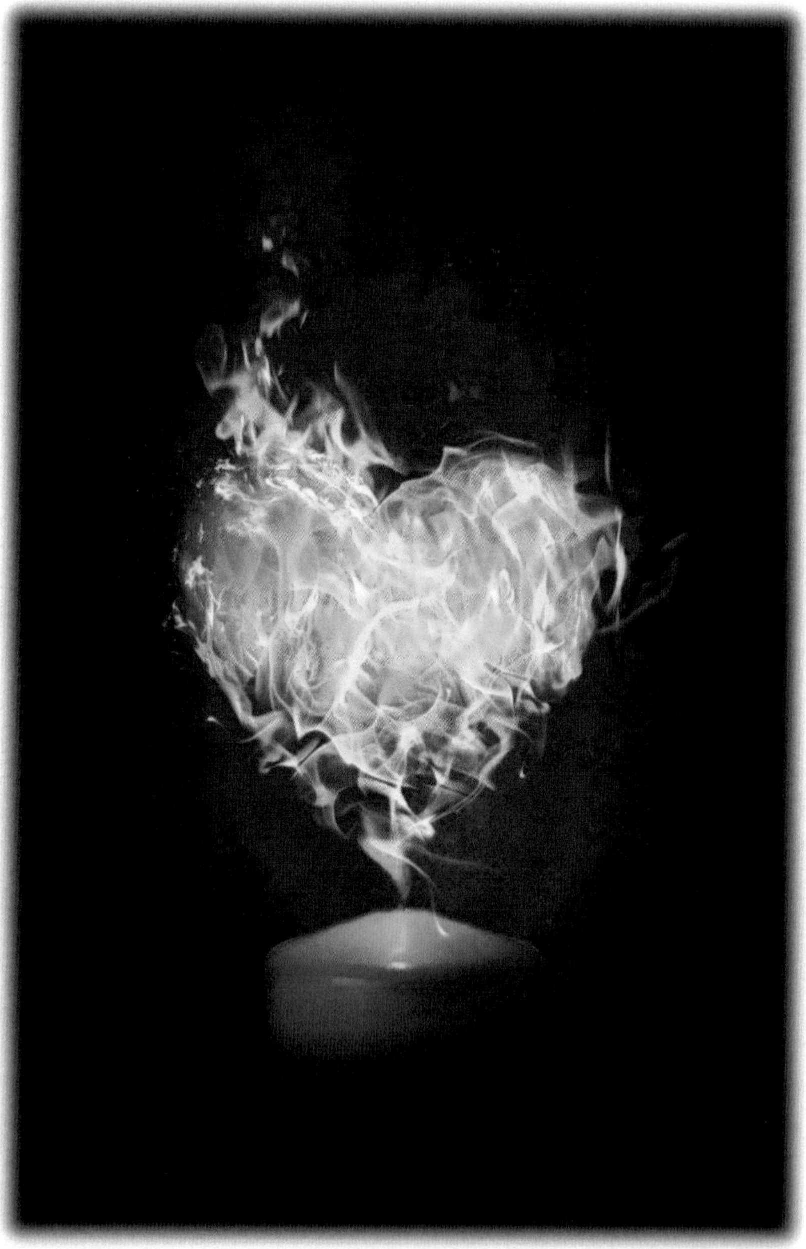

A Good Man Ruins Your Lipstick, Not Your Mascara

As short as this quote is, it hits deep into the core of truth. A good man is focused on making you feel happy by ruining your lipstick with the most intense kisses. He makes her wet all the time when she merely thinks of romantic moments they spend together, let alone when he is by her to kiss her. Abusive men, on the other hand, are more concerned about physical and mental assaults that changes the composition of her makeup. She sobs anytime she thinks of him, and the sight of him brings fear, rather than the awe of respect. Be the man who knows the value of his woman and would not hurt her under any circumstance rather than the monster which his woman sees as a predator of her endangered species.

Don't Deny The Signs, Vibes, And Energy You Feel About Certain People And Certain Situations. If It's Not Right, Its Not Right

The regrets many people make in relationships and marriages today is that of not following the signs. Statistics show that many women who have been abused in their marriage have also been abused during their courtship, but excused it for temper issues or mood disorders. On the other side of the gender coin, men who have experienced non-committal behavior from their spouses or partners admit that they suffered some form of emotional abuse from them in their courting days, expressed in neglect. Hence to avoid having memories of regret as you deserve the best from the relationship, do not take any warning sign for granted in your relationship walk. That way, you'll not be prone to experiencing emotional wreck from bonding with a woman whose heart you do not connect with.

44

When You Can Kick It Without Sex, That Is Real Connection

If sex is removed from the to-do list of most relationships, the couples will realize that there has not been anything more to them than the few minutes of pleasure. Sex sustains one's intimacy, but beyond that, what keeps one going with his or her spouse for a long time is how they fare on life perspectives. Couples should work on understanding their communication styles, nonverbal cues, as well as learning the love language of their spouse. It is not always about sex!

She's The Type That Not Only Catches My Eye But Opens Them

Ever met a lady who kicked your button from the first minute? Every one has. But what about sustaining that to the next level of making you come alive when she is around? Lovely right? The highest level which a man can be at to enjoy peace in a relationship is to be with a woman who helps him discover new horizons. She is the woman to die for – someone who makes you see new potentials in you and is ready to stick to your dream. Such a woman will always be within the romantic radar of her man.

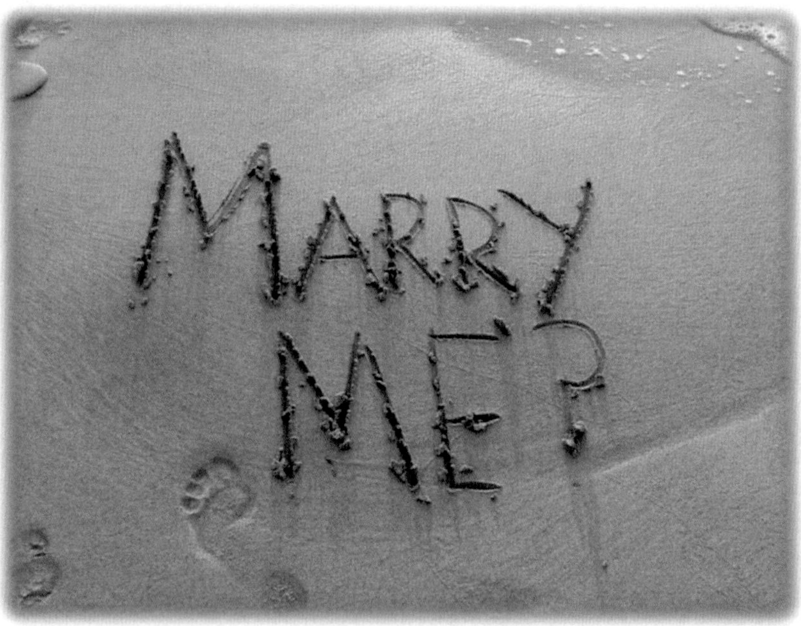
MARRY
ME?

You Deserve A Man Who Is Going To Go Out Of His Way To Make It Obvious He Wants You In His Life

What is the value of love if it is not expressed? But often, lovers hide under "keeping personal life private" to make a relationship secret. You deserve better than that as a woman. Never settle for a man who does not make it evident that he loves you and wants to be with you. Some men have the habit of quitting in their hunt for a woman. Such men should not be given a chance as that behavior reveals what they may do in the face of heated moments in relationships. A real man does not care about anything else but making you see how wanted you are to him in his life.

A Lot Of Men Walk Away Because Y'all Women Was Too Busy Finding Faults In Them, While They Were Busy Overlooking Them

The relationship is all about tolerance. Sadly, a lot of lovers stand on the stool of their faults to point out mistakes of their partners. The needful maturity to get before entering a relationship is to understand that everyone makes a mistake, and more importantly, you are not perfect yourself. Loving becomes a beautiful thing when a person can accommodate the fact that he or she is as liable to error as his or her partners. Many times, women are quick to point out the sins of men so much so that they forget their shortcomings towards men too. Essentially, both parties need to understand their tendencies for weaknesses and be tolerant when they come to have a smooth relationship.

Do I Want You? Yes. Will I Chase You? No.

The dilemma of most men in relationships is having the feeling of desire towards a woman and not being willing to follow it up. Most people let many potential relationships die at the level of attraction as they refuse to move the relationship further. As a man or woman, develop the enthusiasm to go after a man or woman you want. There should be no gender bias on who goes on the love hunt as life is too short not to let one express his or her feelings for fear of being judged.

Everybody Has An Addiction; Mine Just Has To Be You.

The joy of a man or woman in love is to be with their lovers. Nothing means the world to them than that – not even meeting the president. If you are in a union where your partner does not value your presence, or you do not feel any spark when you are around him or her, you might need a reevaluation of the relationship. Your lover has to be someone you are addicted to his or her presence every day; either in thoughts or physical contact. There's just no gainsaying that.

Your Significant Other Is Allowed To Have Meaningful Relationships With Other People. Your Significant Other Is Allowed To Get Things From Those Relationships They Don't Get From You. Demanding You Be The Only Source Of Pleasure And Support In Their Life Is Possessive And Toxic

More often than not, people get angry when their spouse keep friends with other people; especially the opposite sex, when in a relationship with them. Insecurities and mistrust build up in the relationship, and such could make the other partner uncomfortable loving them. Such behavior shows the level of maturity in the person. As a man or woman, you need to understand that your partner will have handsome male friends or beautiful female friends. The love you have for them and the commitment they have shown in the past should let you know that he or she is yours, no matter what. It's nothing to fuss about.

Not All Men Care About How Sexy Your Body Is Or How Pretty You Are, Some Are Waiting To Hear What Comes Out Of Your Mouth

Beautiful women are adored, yet intelligent women are worshipped. Since you want to make up and look chic for yourself as a woman, spend time on personal development to increase charm power. Women who do well in social conversations when they have a chance to express themselves before a crowd tends to be respected or awed. The right conversation also means being courteous in treating another person, avoiding foul language, and saying sweet words to a person. Such behavior is quintessential of how a woman of integrity behaves.

All The Mean Looking Girls Smile As Soon As You Talk To Them

It is often said that the first impression lasts longer. But sometimes, it is risky to go by first impression alone. Some ladies have no smiles on their faces on first-time meetings and are yet golden in the heart. One should not mistake facial expression for personality. She could be going through a bad time, a bad mood, and all. Prove to be the man who can understand a lady's moods by learning to give another shot when next you meet her if the first meeting fails and see the wonder you'll get from that.

A Real Man Understands That Sex Is Not Everything When It Comes To Satisfying His Woman. Comforting Her, Appreciating Her, Respecting Her, Protecting Her, Listening To Her, Understanding Her, Loving Her, Being Loyal & Taking Care Of Her Emotionally Is Also Part Of Pleasing Her

When talks about pleasuring a woman are up for discussion, people get attentive as they think it is all about erotic pleasure. A woman's pleasure principle is more complex than just that. It is all about giving her a sense of respect, attentiveness, protection, understanding, loyalty, love, and care. As a man, even if you give her the best sex in the world, she still won't be satisfied if she does not see more commitment from you in the listed areas. Sex occupies a small percentage of the 24-hour clock, hence what you do beyond the sex time frame is what maintains the relationship and not the sex alone.

Not All Men Come For One Thing! Some Men Come To Heal, Repair, Uplift And Restore

It is a psychological conditioning that most ladies have that once a man comes for them, they feel they want to prey on them for their body gratifications and leave – just like the other men! But the truth is no matter what experience of trusting men may have taught you, and you need to understand that men are not all the same. Of a fact, some men come with vain intentions.

On the other hand, others come to heal, repair, and fix the missing piece in your soul right back. For this reason, you need to position yourself for the coming of such a man, lest you miss him. It all starts by a cognitive reawakening – tell yourself every day, "not all men come for one thing! Some men come to heal, repair, uplift, and restore."

That Cologne Is Going To Get Her Attention Before The Fancy Belt

The expression places the importance of good grooming skills for the man, much more than what he wears. That is to lay to rest the erroneous perception most men have that women love people with expensive things. While that is a half-truth, the full truth remains that women are also endeared by the smell of the cologne that a man uses. Hence, a man ought to make sure to use good smell appeal to get the attention of his woman and keep her remembering her whenever she perceives the scent.

Feed Her Ears With Honesty, Her Eyes Loyalty, And Drown Her Heart Inconsistency

One vice women hate in a man is lying. A woman wants to know that she is with a man who cannot cheat on her; a man that does not means words with discordant actions. Her eyes, ears, and heart need to sense the same amount of energy from you. For this reason, you need to be in love with your woman genuinely. Loving your woman genuinely will help have the same identity in her eyes, heart, and ears. It does not take much from you to get to such a point. Just by loving her genuinely and being forthrightly in love with her, she will have the same picture of a loving man when she sees or hears you as you'll be a permanent incision in her heart.

"You Had Her With Your Words And Lost Her With Your Actions"

The easiest to endear beings in the world has to be a human female. They have got a strong affinity for words that the words you say can make or mar her at an instant. That is why it is possible to sweep a woman off her feet on a first-time-basis conversation. Men who can wield words eloquently often have it good with women. The problem, however, is that most men do not always continue with such flow after she has given him a chance. Their words speak louder than their action, and they leave her, wondering if they have not made a mistake choosing the wrong person. As a man, learn to follow up your words with the appropriate action. There are things you'll do for a woman, and she will know you love her; it is not always about saying it.

Find A Woman With A Brain

Pageantry business has taught that beauty is not all about physical looks but also about intellectual comportment. For this reason, the one with the smoothest of faces or abundance of curves sometimes does not win. Your intellectual comportment as a woman matters, and that is what most men are on the lookout for in their relationship partners. A man wants a woman that he can present to his friends in a social gathering and be relaxed that she will overawe them in a conversation. Hence as a man, you have to be more focused on the intellectual framework of a woman than her physical looks. If not for any reason, but for the sad reality that beauty is vain, hold on to what will outlast beauty and your years together.

If She Eats Her French Fries With A Fork, She's Probably Not Going To Do That Thing You Like

A woman who shows a high-level standard of behavior is likely to be fastidious. She may be principled to a fault, and that could get you annoyed at times, especially if you are the conservative type. Such a woman, however, is a plus for principle loving men. Hence if you know you want a woman who is a bit flexible with rules, go for a woman who is just like you. In that decision comes your happiness.

I'm Basically A Hopeless Romantic Who Has Standards

Sometimes, being a person of professional charisma does not mean you have to be all serious in your relationship. You need to get on your freaky level at times to spice things up in your relationships. You and your lover can engage in reading or viewing sexual materials together, telling her dirty jokes, among other things. Sex is never enough because these little things add up at the end of the day in boosting your love life. It also follows that just because one has a dirty mind does not mean that one lacks principles or standards. It is part of the romance package, not an earmark of a philanderer.

When A Woman Is Treated Right, She Is Naturally Submissive

Many times, men are often likely to think that women do not respond well to care, and they take men who show care as weak. A woman wants a man that can show strength and give her security when she is in love with him. Since she wants this, she also values being treated right and so, and you have to learn to do that as a man. Make her feel loved as much as you can. Be by her, stand for her, and love her as much as you love her. That way, she will submit to you whether you are an alpha male or not.

Having A Crush On Someone Only Lasts 4 Months, If It Lasts Longer, You Are In Love

Funny but real; feelings of love last much longer than that of infatuations. Several things often infatuate a person. Could be the way she talks, her accents, her sex appeal, or so many other things. All these are not strong enough to pass as love hence they fade away in time. However, love is more intimate than crushing on someone. You do not even need to interact with the person you have a crush on to be infatuated. Love is expressed in action and communication; hence if what one feels does not last long enough, it can only be a crush and not a romance.

The Right Man Will Want To Be More To You Than Just Your Man; He'll Want To Be Your Best Friend, Your Confidant And The One Person And The One Person In This World To Never Disappoint You

Being in love has many responsibilities. It involves being everything to the woman whom one loves. One must be willing to be her lover, confidant, brother, friend, sexual partner, best friend amid other roles. It's a woman's dream to find a man who means the world to her. Women in relationships with men who cannot show these other commitments apart from bearing the tag "lover" end up having friends who shower them with such responsibility. You have to be all things to her to keep her. Doing all these for her will most likely culminate in her trust for you as she will always cherish you both in your presence and absence.

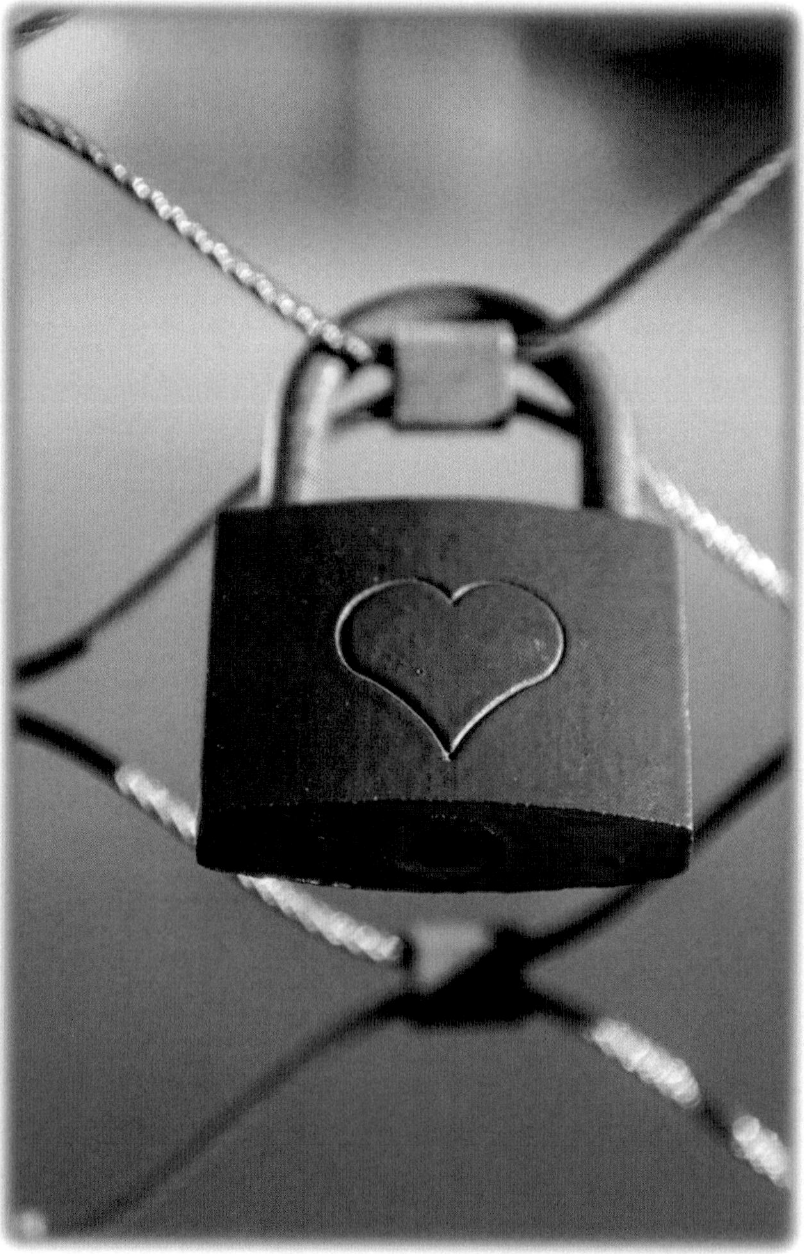

Long Term Consistency Beats Short Term Intensity

Nothing compares to being committed to someone over long periods, despite signs of not yielding to one. It never goes unrewarded. Many men flag off their overtures on a woman, only to cut it short midway when there seems to be no positive response to the woman whose heart they seek. What such men do not realize is that most times, the way to a woman's heart takes time. She may take long before seeing your worth and reciprocating the same energy which you give her, hence the reason why you need to persevere on the road of love till you become what you dream of becoming. Short-term intensity can also mean infatuation or even lust – ephemeral things. One should give feelings time to be assessed if they are borne out of lust and passion. That way, there will be no possibility of making the wrong decisions.

71244322R10051

Made in the USA
Columbia, SC
25 August 2019